Skal

Poetry Books by Gary Geddes

GARY GEDDES

Skaldance

GOOSE LANE

Simultaneously published in the UK by Peterloo Poets.

Edited by Ross Leckie.
Cover painting "Black Ladder" © Martin Honisch, 1985.
Cover and interior design by Julie Scriver.
Printed in Canada by AGMV Marquis.
10 9 8 7 6 5 4 3 2

National Library of Canada Cataloguing in Publication

Geddes, Gary, 1940-
Skaldance / Gary Geddes.

Poems.
ISBN 0-86492-387-2

1. Sailing — Poetry. 2. Orkney (Scotland) — Poetry. I. Title.

PS8563.E3S43 2004   C811'.54   C2003-906697-5

Published with the financial support of the Canada Council for the Arts,
the Government of Canada through the Book Publishing Industry Development
Program, and the New Brunswick Culture and Sports Secretariat.

Goose Lane Editions
469 King Street
Fredericton, New Brunswick
CANADA E3B 1E5
www.gooselane.com

This book is for Win Bogaards
and Wynn Thomas

Contents

Four

His mute lines are but a distant flute.
Izzat Ghazzawi

It is still, thank God, harder to tell lies in art than in life.
Peter Perrin

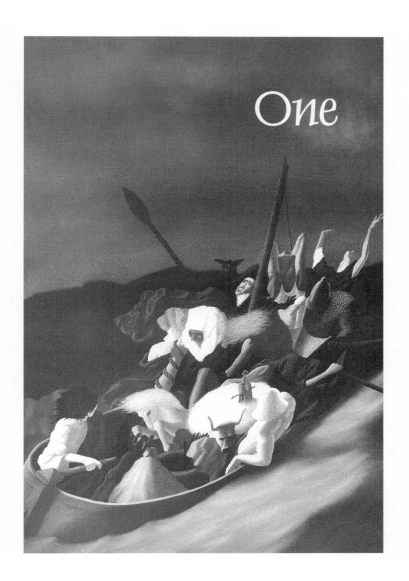

One

Back Eddies

So the return, the ragged shoreline white with rage,
wind salting the fields, topsoil flying, the whole island
turned turtle. We're crofters still, colour TV on the
built-in flagstone shelf, rusty half-ton moored outside the
floating bog-house, wheels submerged to the axles in mud.
A flutter of tourists replaces the herring stocks, oil and its
slick operatives spreading out across the Pentland Firth.
Tanker adrift, engine room aflame. Toxic cargo, she
thought, ignition point lower than a rat's ass.

She stays at the Pierowall Hotel on Westray where a
karaoke interlude is in progress, islanders drinking
themselves legless, songward. Lauren and Sammo buy
two rounds, invite her over for coffee the next day. Sammo
has tried guiding tourists but the bills went unpaid. Rigs
or marine work in Aberdeen; Lauren and six kids at home,
with e-mail and maybe the hairdressing she's trained for
but never used. Sees the wreck along the road before she
hears the news. More career changes, abrupt alterations in
the shoreline where, for millennia, angled slabs thrust up
from the spume, judicial as carving knives.

After checking out the home place, doing her graveyard
roll call of Pottingers, Mowats and Houries, all paid-up
members of that exclusive underground club, she stops at
the Broch of Gurness to put it in perspective. Between
flagstone walls a pale blue vinyl pup tent has been pitched.
The solitary camper, face a deeper, bruised blue, warms
his hands over a propane stove fired up for tea. A Czech

student working at a health care facility in Inverness, part-time. Homesick and finding what, reciprocity with the dead? She excuses herself. She's looking for a landscape as blighted and surreal as the aftermath of love, a Dieppe or Vimy Ridge of the heart. She thinks she's found it: no trees, just scars, and monuments to periodic invasion.

P.O.W.

He grew remote, acquired a language
I could not decipher. My airman, my high-
flyer, cryptic, hieratic, more complicated
than Linear B, or the Dresden Codex.

Demented not demotic, and no Rosetta Stone
to tap. I failed to crack his code,
its glyphs and glygers, the Dead Sea
Scroll of love I languished in. I regressed,

mute in the face of shifting vowels, lost
consonants. Tore my hair, mouthed vows,
cursed this vain enigma in his cuneiform.
Dismissed, of course, as menopause,

the rash that formed upon my belly
proof enough. And sleep, that famous
balm, exploded in my face. Other things
on his mind: war, unfinished business

in Dundee. Or was it Dunsinane? I was one
witch too many, no Orkney wood to order
wrapped as camouflage. I'd ruined his precious
furlough; the poems he'd planned to write

were out the window. I could kiss the ass
of my Italian gardener, for all he cared,
stepping into his plane. And so I did,
as well as all his other parts. One by one,

I felt my unvoiced cells rejuvenate; the itch
migrated south. I couldn't get enough
of him, his crazy grin, the ridge of dirt
beneath his nails. Even the quaint

Catholic saints he painted on his tin roof's
corrugations performed sweet ministries
— coleslaw phonemes, pasta pictographs —
till I too, earthbound, human, got my wings.

Companion Piece

We sit in the rented car, heat turned up,
while tourists file past. Excitement
keeps them smiling, warm. A small child
rides on her father's shoulders, gloved
hands forming a speckled headband

just above his eyes. Henry is grumpy.
Money and privilege make him think
the weather should oblige, as I oblige,
his every whim. Well, not *every*. There
are limits, even for the wealthy man's

companion. I've packed scarf and gloves,
lunch prepared at the wayside hotel
by Mrs. Sigurdson, cucumbers sliced thin
and spread with Dijonnaise, a hybrid
he encountered at the Jewish delicatessen

in Westmount and insists on packing
with his jar of peanut butter. You'd think
he was the Earl of Sandwich on a jaunt
to Warwickshire. Today he's content
to have me read brochures, leave the sites

to others. He'll know as much as anyone
at dinner, without discomfort or
exertion. The words blur, I have to read
each sentence several times to catch its
drift. Mrs. Roach (pronounced in the French

way as Roche) from Cincinnati waxed
prosaic about the burial mound we'd
skipped yesterday. I couldn't breathe,
she gushed, mushy peas caught in gaps
of her teeth. Claustrophobia, don't

you know; even on planes, I can't sit
in the middle seat without starting to
hyperventilate. I could see Henry tense up,
chew each mouthful of beef thirty times
to keep his tongue occupied, his restraint

uncharacteristic, I thought. By now
the windows have fogged up and I can't see
the path to the neolithic village
or the receding shoreline. Just Henry's
sour expression and his own receding

hair, all that's left white and fringed
like the ridge of dirty snow
that builds all winter along sidewalks
in Montreal. Panic catches
in my throat, my voice falters.

I'm thirty years younger, not ready
for the shelf or geriatric ward.
My oils gather dust, my children
drift out of touch. There are things
I want to see that words can't conjure.

I want to feel the bite of cold, colour
in my cheeks as I remove my parka.
The uncertainty of what to buy
at Provigo, whether the bus will stop
in a snow storm, the heating

system collapse, water pipes burst.
Right on cue, Henry has to pee. I turn
on the defrost fan, shift out of park.
I could open the door, take my foot off
the brake, and step into history.

The Lady's Not for Burning

I grew up on the island, near Rysa,
at Greengairs Cottage, not far
from the Waters of Hoy. I was twenty-seven,
my Andrew off for a year
in the whaling. When the blood
did not flow, I walked
into the sea — it didn't take
a genius to predict public
reaction. Alas, as my lungs
binged and no gills sprouted,
some well-meaning fool
rescued me. I had to try again,
this time with a length of rope
in the barn. The letter *i* added
to barn gives you bairn; that's
why it's dangerous to play
with words. Simple recipe:
desire, a touch of comfort,
then the two of us at the end
of our respective tethers.
The year, 1779. Interred, after
debate, in unconsecrated ground,
the clergy and lairds for once
in agreement. Out of sight
for 150 years, until two crofters
named Robb struck gold
in an Orkney bog.
While postman and police
looked on in amazement
at my preserved flesh,

revulsion and longing
registered in slack jaw
and hungry eye, the necklace
of hemp disintegrated
alongside my peat-stained
arms, black hair. More
heat still in Betty
Corrigall than in the slabs
they stacked and baked
in sunlight. At least
that's what His Majesty's
Best thought, planting
their telegraph poles
beyond the naval base
at Lyness. I was the first
naked woman many of them
had seen; curiosity aroused
and sated, poles intact, they
laid me again to rest, somewhat
the worse for air. A lance
corporal, with pimples and a skin
disease, penned a new species
of verse in my honour
and tacked it to the coffin lid:
Her name is Betty Corrigall,
her fate was something 'orrible.
The "Lady" of Hoy
who had sex with a boy
was considered completely incorrigible.
I never had so much
attention while alive; and I paid
for what little there was
dearly. Andrew gave me

a whale's tooth and an illustrated
book of verses that belonged
to his learned mother,
who had drowned years earlier
without even trying. How
can a woman sensitive enough
to hang herself be so
cynical? Despite opinions
to the contrary, you learn a few things
in the course of two centuries
underground, unless you're
brain-dead. I wasn't ashamed
or fearful, just realistic;
and I loved Andrew too much
to subject him to public
ridicule. I savoured my
privacy. Spiteful Christians
or lecherous farm boys
with broken nails and cabbage faces
I can handle, but sentimental
humanists with eulogies
and concrete markers, definitely
not. A few eons more and
this mortal coil will be combustible
as peat. I could burn like Joan,
released from my island
of flesh, free at last
to know everything, whirl
among planets, bivouac
in the hearts and minds
of those who love
and murder us. Truth is,
I'm a bit of a homebody,

untroubled by cosmic
ambitions, fixed agendas.
I prefer the dust of Hoy
from which I came,
the offshore winds that
breathed life into me.
Nearby's the patch of grass
that bore the imprint
of my back and bum
for days. I sometimes
watch the play of light
and shadow on Andrew's
forehead as he sends
singing into me his seed,
his crazy, grateful
smile. No thanks, I think
I'll just stay put.

Blood Work

It had to do with making
tents, tight canvas triangles
used by soldiers in wartime.
Afterwards, we diversified
and switched to awnings,

various sizes of marquee.
Success was wasted on Daddy.
He took his Bentley
out of the garage once a week
to wax, but never drove it

anywhere. I got as far away
as possible without resorting
to Toronto or Hobart.
Orkney absorbed all the pain
I could muster. I always use

canvas for oils, cut
and stretched over the lids
of Jap-orange crates, old
window frames. The winds
on Harray blow right up

your kazoo. You can't define
the sky, or even catch it
the same two days running.
I wanted billboards
to paint, sides of derelict

buildings. I met a Belgian
on the train to Inverness,
his briefcase bulging
with picturesque harbours
and quaint pinched faces

he flogged from Westray
to Brussels. Back home
markets were glutted, clientele
bored with familiar views.
The risks art required

he couldn't afford, not yet.
I watched the sun rise
from his temporary digs
on the third floor. The
sloped ceiling reminded me

of Daddy's tents; so, too,
the slope of flesh above
his shaggy genitals. Fuck
me first, then paint me,
I said, smearing myself

across his chest. I thought
he'd faint to see the blood
tattoo I'd given him.
With strangers I'm okay;
no need for fine print,

my blatant lust convenient
cover. A few innocent
drinks, then the sluices open
and I drown. Why blame
mother for not wanting

her children? Less a matter
of hostility than indifference,
her attentions elsewhere.
Trimming canvas, buying
expensive dresses she'd

never get to wear. Money
doesn't guarantee admission.
While Mommy primped
and played the lady,
Daddy plucked his banjo

in the basement, key
to the wine cellar beside
him on the workbench.
All he ever wanted was
to entertain, his fingers

tracing invisible strings
as Formby's florid face
glistened on stage, lips
belting out the words to
"Mr. Wu" and "Blackpool

Rock." Even straining
in full harness, the Belgian
couldn't make me come,
though I blessed him for
his efforts. Antidepressants

take the edge off. You feel
it happen in another room.
Don't get me wrong, it's
not frustrating; just a little
sad, remote, a faded

memory or photograph
you know had special
meaning. Though I scoffed
at his miniatures, laid
end-to-end they formed

an epic panorama of such
scope and disturbing
detail, I purchased the lot
and wept for days each
time I looked at them.

Periwinkle

Not the first indicator by a long
shot, but it registers seven on my
Richter scale. Richter mortis.
Periwinkles too, raw salt taste
of the North Atlantic. The same

as those we used to order at bars
in Soho, imported to New York
by air, packed in ice. Alfred is
speaking to me in the burial mound.
Not Maes Howe, the smaller one

where a sign gives you directions
for picking up the key. We crawled
in with flashlights — the English call
them torches — but have switched them
off and sit in total darkness, cold

earth, cold stones, drawing the August
heat from our backs and thighs.
We cycled all morning, stopping
at a guest house seven kilometres
outside Kirkwall, ostensibly for tea

but really to use the facilities.
Either they have epic bladders,
since there are no protective
groves and roadside bushes,
or a low consumption of liquids,

these mad Orcadians. If you think
this is bad, I said to Alfred
over toasted muffins, imagine
Sir Gawain setting out from here
on horseback and in full armour.

He must have had to urinate —
but what a production. I was
about to describe the cacophony
a medieval knight would make
dismounting, when the hostess

delivered our platter of steamed
periwinkles. Just as well, since
Alfred was somewhere else,
in his proverbial, and apparently
portable, brown study. His

greying shoulder-length hair
brought out the Dutch — I liked
to think of it as the Scandinavian
— in him. Penoka farmboy
turned scholar of Old English

and Old Norse. Periwinkles
had been an afterthought.
Indulgences, we called them,
a small reward for healthy
living. The black spiralled shells

resembled tiny spinning tops.
When we emerged from tea
a tethered goat was chewing
the saddle of Alfred's bike.
My eyes are trying to adjust

to the total absence of light.
I can feel my enlarged pupils
founder, drown in darkness.
We could stay here forever,
Alfred says, save ourselves a lot

of bother. His voice reaches out
to touch me, almost palpable
in the shapeless dark of the burial
mound. I couldn't speak even
if I tried. I'm breathing

too quickly. It's all I can do
not to flick on the plastic switch
of the flashlight. Alfred says:
He probably had on stainless
steel. What? The single word

I utter comes out as a low groan.
Gawain, he says after a minute,
the armour. I squeeze the rubber
grip of the flashlight. It feels
like the handles of my bicycle,

only thicker. The periwinkle,
Alfred continues, scratching
a match on the stone wall
as he lights a cigarette,
is also a plant, a species of scrub

with light blue starry flowers
of the genus Vinca, related
to the Old English *peruinca*
and the Latin *pervinca*. Oddly,
though associated with the verb

to conquer, its flowers were
often woven in the form of garlands
that were placed on the heads
of those about to be executed.
Thus its nickname, flower

of death. In Holland, according
to Pliny, it grows all year round.
How incongruous, since Dutch
justice is notoriously seasonal.
The fiery ash of his cigarette

dances somewhere to the left
of his voice. I feel in my hip
pocket the key to our holiday-
special do-it-yourself sepulchre.
I can also feel slow current

discharging from the dry-cell
batteries as my walking dictionary
husband, his tone shifting, says:
It also functions as a figure
of speech, meaning the fairest,

someone exquisite, in the pink
of perfection, and is a term
of endearment for a girl
or woman, as in *Forever*
shall I love thee, Periwinkle.

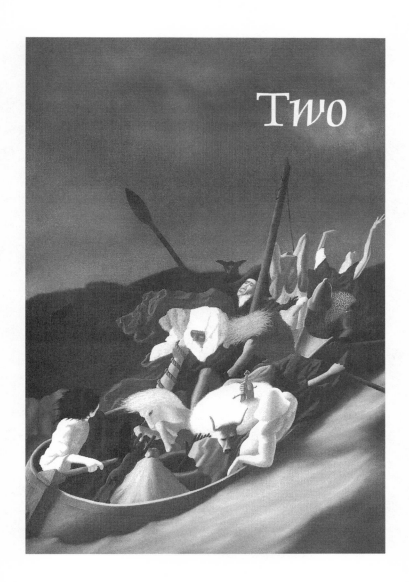

Two

Wilderness Factor

Isbister's gone, six years in the skin trade
earns a visit home. Divine accounting —
leave it to Hudson Bay. Each sabbath year
thou shalt rest, return home via Montreal,
Orkney, bearing trade goods in excess
of ten thousand pounds, skins for fat burghers,
London's la-di-dahs. Two magpies
tear at the remains of a dead muskrat
on the south bank of the river, below
the stockade where canoes push off,
laden with bales amidships. He never
looks back, or turns to wave, the shapes
of his dark children already lost in fog
and river vapours. No swish of crinolines

here or carriages lined up along the quay
as on the day he steps ashore in Kirkwall,
a man of property, elder and provider.
No longer, as his name trumpets, John
of the east homestead, he's slipped
into history, pre-booked passage a sign
of grace. Too polite to ask, his wife
can smell the wilderness that oozes
from his pores, see the treed creatures
stirring in his eyes, the ghostly trace
of dreams that curl in smoke around his pipe
and beard. She knows the blunt anchor
he lowers in her stagnant pool won't hold;
it will drift, be weighed, found wanting,

she can imagine what. Another pale child
to fill the spaces where there are no words,
no eloquence of touch. A seven-league
soul starving in its leghold trap
of flesh. She feels it suck the marrow
from her bones; her tidal estuary's
almost dry. But still his ship decamps
on schedule at dawn. Shadowy forms
engulf him at the rail, stretch the sheets
to full capacity. She feels the muscles
in her wrist contract to wave, but something —
is it pride? — causes her to pause. Too late,
the ship is swinging on a starboard
tack, the fog moves in, Isbister's gone.

Down for the Count

The word *relationship*. It conjures
so little of the intricate urges
& negotiations that keep two people
hostage under a single roof
without having recourse to carnage

or Kraft Dinners. Kidnapper
and victim may be said to stand
in a certain relationship. So, too,
employee and boss. It's politics,
biology. After we'd seen the movie

of *The English Patient*, I took her out
for cabbage rolls and perogies
in the north end of Edmonton.
There were no Hungarian restaurants,
so we pretended the count was Ukrainian.

My problem: when I read a book
or see a movie, I identify with every
character. I'm saint and cad,
jilter and jilted, no action or sentiment
beyond my range of possibility.

It's not just scary; it's exhausting.
She wanted to know where things
stood. *What things?* I said. This was
not the right answer. A drop of blood
appeared in the outstretched palm

of her left hand. Was it a fine passion?
Would the trail of flickering candles
lead to a quiet consummation
amongst repotted gladiola plants
and defused bombs? My grandfather

emigrated in 1907 from the Orkneys
to Cortes Island, where he cleared
twenty-five acres and tried subsistence
farming. He used to take me fishing
in a fourteen-foot clinker with a

three-and-a-half horsepower Briggs
and Stratton engine that smoked
terribly because the rings were shot.
I got seasick, but I liked his stories
and the smell of his Old Chum

tobacco. He told me about Colonel
Galway, a remittance man
who wore a monocle and dressed
to the nines, though if you looked
closely you could detect the threadbare

status of the cloth. He was a crack
shot and used to ask local *coves*
out for a shoot when he was feeling
boastful or effusive. His dog,
also refined, tried to mate

with the neighbour's Labrador,
a huge creature named Lady Rowena
of Lorelei — Rona for short —
and the colonel would always say:
Majah, get away from that bitch!

The kids who tended his lawn
were told they'd find garden tools
in the gazebo out back. They opened
the rattan door and screamed
as the stuffed Bengal tiger, reclining

on a wicker loveseat, flashed
them a smile. Colonel and the Mrs.
bathed in the shallows, current
massaging their liverish torsos.
When the cheques stopped coming,

Colonel G. cut his grandchild's
throat as she lay in the crib,
then tried, without success,
to take his own life. I still can't
get a grip on that one; it makes me

feel as useless as Caravaggio without
thumbs. Somehow I've derailed
her life, taken her hostage.
While I think of body curves
fading into the light and shadow

of sand dunes, she's busy rehearsing
the Stockholm syndrome. The perogies,
though cold, were still tasty, mashed
potatoes in a jacket. A dinner jacket.
She was not amused. I thought of rods,

lures, combustion engines, my
grandfather drowned just off the entrance
to Kettle Harbour. He always resented
that Manson got to Cortes first
and had a Landing named after him.

Subtext

When I first went on board
in Bremerhaven, the quarters
were cramped, the bunks narrow
envelopes you couldn't turn
in. I wanted to run screaming
from the deadly intimacy
of this space. But there were
latrines to scrub, quarters
to tidy, and laundry — O Christ! —

the laundry. A change of
clothes at midday, not just
for officers. Stains verboten,
court martial for crumbs.
We inched between the sunken
vessels they used as barriers,
hum of the diesels scarcely
audible. I watched the muscles
twitch in Heinrich's cheek

as he leaned into the bulkhead,
a white oil rag waterfalling
from the pocket of his blue
overalls. Click. Click. Click.
The Old Man at the scope,
his elegant hands conducting
the operation. A short blast
of power with the rudder full
to port would straighten us

out. Scrape of barnacles
on the starboard side, then
we were clear. Clear to deliver
our billet-doux, post-haste,
into the belly of the English
cruiser. Highwater slack;
tea time, lads, high tea.
In twenty minutes the tide
would turn, current surge

through the gap. All I could think of
were two cans of sauerkraut
Heinrich and I in disguise
had purchased the day before
in Stromness. Don't let Jerry
get a whiff of this, he said
in a Cockney accent as he quit
the store. The proprietor's laugh
blended with the tinkling bell.

Inspecting the Chickens

Beachcombing's just as good
a training ground for the buyer
of books. You learn to keep an eye

on tides, weather, migrations,
disasters at sea. It's the martins,
myrtles, and sand-devils

I look for, the little surprises
and whirlwinds that walk into
your life and — presto! — everything

is changed. I was reading Borges'
Ficciones and making a dent
in a bottle of contraband Madeira

when she asked for the books
on birds and birding. I offended her
by laughing, not at the question

but at Borges' Pierre Menard,
who postulates a modern rewrite
of the *Quixote* that is "identical

yet superior" to the original.
The rest, forgive me, is history,
the kind more often obscured

than illuminated by books.
Real toads in imaginary gardens,
as the American poet says.

I want to correct the impression
left by Señor Borges in his *Book
of Sand*. We met in '68, not

in Buenos Aires but in London,
outside the Methodist Church
in Westminster, where he was

lecturing to an overflow audience.
I squeezed in before they closed
the doors and stood near the back

during the performance. I was
at loose ends, my bird-lady having
dumped me after a protracted

disagreement. I'll skip the details.
Suffice to say, she did not take kindly
to the volume of my daily

libations. I wish we'd never left
St. Margaret's Hope, she announced
grim-faced as she stepped into a coach

on Track 5 at King's Cross. I tried
to convince her to stay on, that things
would improve. I was ghostly white,

my legs trembling from the
accumulated poisons, but I wanted
to put a good face on it: "Hope is

not so easily discarded, my angel."
If only I could make her laugh
I'd know what to do next. The train

was pulling out. She kissed me
firmly on the mouth, then hauled
back and slugged me, so I collapsed

into the arms of a passing porter.
At the front of the church, Borges
explained how he'd been promoted

from the post of Chicken Inspector
to head the Argentine National Library
but had gone blind the same year.

Was it projection, or did he seem
to be gripping the sides of the pulpit
like a drenched helmsman

in a storm? I groaned. A cripple
offered me his seat in the back row.
As I staggered towards the exit

I heard Borges say he'd taken up
the study of Old English
to celebrate his blindness. Don't ask

why, but I started to weep. Nothing
would console me, but to shake
this sightless seer's hand. Scales

fell from my eyes. I developed
a thirst for fiction, biography, all
the riches of Aladdin's cave

at my disposal. I never looked
back. I wrote letters to Borges
from St. Margaret's Hope

where I raised Rhode Island Reds
and ran the local W.E.A. branch
with books from my personal

library. We discussed the principle
of randomness, Heraclitus,
stepping twice in the same

euphemism. I used the image of sand
in an hourglass to make my point
that movement alone underlies

our awareness of time. Underwrites
would be more accurate, he replied,
since time, like so much else,

is an agreed-on fiction, a literary
device. If grains of sand sufficed,
he'd visit me in Orkney. I sent

by return post my *Book of Sand*,
constructed from a damaged bible.
I carved a rectangle in the warped

pages, inserted a cigar box
full of Grim Ness sand, then
rebound the volume meticulously

in leather with marbled end-
papers. Sand contains all narrative,
I wrote, erasing footprints, absorbing

blood and tears, covering the remains
of expeditions, cities. It's purer
than words, which are static, fixed,

time-sensitive. Run the grains of sand
through your fingers and you'll
possess all knowledge, the complete

history of man. I was as pleased
with my spiel as with my gift
and watched the post twice daily

for a reply. Finally, a postcard
arrived from Giovanni to say
the master was dead. I laughed —

to think the man who'd translated
all those books and fantastical tales
would acknowledge death. No

mention was made of my gift.
Years later, I came across a copy
of his own *Book of Sand* in a shop

in Aberdeen. How did he know,
being blind, I was tall, nondescript
and blond? An inspired guess,

no doubt, another universe
in a grain of sand. I forgave him
for making my fictional self

a Presbyterian whose pinched
soul is more allied to barter
than infinity. A Bible salesman?

A broker in truth, perhaps, but not
a hawker of Bibles. The beleaguered
saint who knocked me for a loop

at King's Cross Station has called
me many things in her time:
a lush, a fanatic, a fool. But even she

would not have stooped so low
as that. Walking along the beach
together in a soft rain, she takes

my elbow in her hand. We can
see the outline of Swona, where it
punctuates the stretch of

Pentland Firth, and stop to examine
a sand-martin's nest in the high
bank. The small brown migratory

creatures have lined the hole
with twigs and sea moss. She has on
a pair of wellies, canary yellow,

I picked up in London on a whim
during my last buying trip. She
kicks the wet sand and sends

a spray of minute grains cascading
into the slack waters. I take
her face in my hands and kiss

her eyes, feeling the closed
lids move beneath my lips. How come
you're so beautiful, after all

these years? She smiles, cold
hands moving inside my jacket
as she says: You can always

trust a blind man, a lover of rare
books and chickens, to pull
the wool over your eyes.

Graffiti

White legs disappearing over a rise
left their imprint on the mind, like
fingers pressed in flesh of the upper
thigh. Inhabitants, few and ragged,

might have been subdued, quickly
dispatched, recreation and release
seldom denied a company of men.
But food was primary; we could

spill our seed later among breakers
and sea-wrack. Leave just enough to keep
the gaunt islanders alive, rooting
among cabbages. Supply and demand.

No slash and burn for Skril's crew,
smoking remains visible miles astern.
My shipmates boasted doing it in boats,
on horseback, even in an open grave.

Likely stories, I thought. Vulgar,
not only content predictable, but the very
rasp and reek. Guttural, beer-laden.
I laughed. More pleasure to be found

in writing down the words than in the chase.
A grave admission. Cryptic notations
all too appropriate in this steamy
grotto, site of a loss I could not voice.

Me? I was fifteen, wall-eyed, a virgin,
too large for my own good. I took delight
in thrusting bones through the blunt hole
we hacked in the roof of the burial

mound. Not a single weapon or gem
to adorn the dead was found in the heap
of grinning skulls. Have they no style,
no decorum? Skril growled, thrusting out

his lower jaw. While Loki and Bjorn
duelled with a pair of glistening
femurs, I, Olaf, scratched my name
where no one else could reach.

Song of the Foreskin

Info, data, stats, when what I want
is the lean dirge of departure. The last
cry from the Stromness ship, a keening

so plaintive it moves like fog across the sea
and up the tarred pilings of the pier
into my bones. As if song might sustain

us, fill the void, stitch elegance into rags.
Margaret, siblings in steerage, left behind
to please a childless uncle. The stark

profile in the porthole, as the blunt
stern of the steamer inches past, recalls
a cameo, a coin. Family secrets:

x-files, subpoenas, restricted documents.
Fake brick siding on the shed out back
where blood leapt bright from the torn string

of a boy's foreskin. The crude fridge wears
its coiled brain on top for all the world to see.
Rain pisses down, a westerly drives cumulus

up the inlet. Mountains in the distance
transmogrify from green to brown to the grey
of weathered cedar boards. The heart,

its mythic inheritance, an ancient fuel pump
worn on the sleeve, corded and hanging
like a curse or amulet. I tried to sketch

the Abbey ruins, temples the Duncombes
constructed at Rievaulx. Neo-classical,
as out of place as they were out of scale.

I wasn't Wordsworth, I had no patience
with what he calls sublime. Not so Margaret's
gift, a wooden gauge my grandfather

carved to inscribe a cutting line on boards.
Houses I'd not set foot in. My fingers
graze the threaded shank, the interlocking

nuts of the scriber. Its sharpened point
penetrates the callus of my thumb. Music,
inscriptions, tools, aught that joins us.

Three

Orkneyinga

You don't expect them so far north,
these tenders of cabbage. Vikings
yes, their consuming lusts, sacking
the land for all it's worth,

leaving in their doleful wake
shards of oar and sail, ironic
burial-mound inscriptions, runic,
crude: *This place would take*

even snooty Ingeborg down a notch
or two. Let the grey friars plant
to excess, then prune to scant
numbers; or lean on shovels, watch

sodden as squat bay ships arrive
to take on water, provisions,
men. The storm, its latest revisions
of the coastline, reveals a hive

of underground activity.
Did neolithic warrens house
your smoke-stained forebears, espouse
communal living? Piety

in stark relief: standing stones
are history's broken teeth. Seeds
germinate, the Armada bleeds
north in disarray, Neptune's throne

witnesses the orchestral descent
of the Kaiser's fleet. Italian
prisoners of war imagine
freedom, baroque, in the rent

veil of a painted Quonset's Sistine
grace. And you, authorial stance
eroded by impish time, chance
on cabbage, blue, crisp, cool, pristine.

Skara Brae

I was gathering dried dung
and driftwood for the hearth
when I saw the great tree
snagged on a string of rocks
offshore, its branches tall
as god-stones, thrust up
out of the water. My basket

safe on high ground, I shed
my skins and waded out
for a closer look. I'd spent
first light three steps
behind Yold, placing seeds
into the shallow furrows
his ard cut in the moist

earth. I made a joke
about our reversed roles
he didn't understand.
Yold is lame, the gash
on his leg from the jagged
flagstone slow to heal.
I stanched the flow of blood

with the flesh of a puffball,
then applied fermented
leaves. I admire the way
he uses his injury to justify
the afternoons inside,
away from women
and cabbages, grinding

tools from whalebone,
gannet's leg. I gather eggs
from shag and guillemot
with his sisters, lie in wait
for otter, for him. Yold, Yold,
I think, watching the seventh
wave break, you've no idea,

none. The ancients
I consulted say your eyes
will open with the solstice;
meanwhile, I bide my time,
scan the sea for secrets.
Water presses close
against my skin, insinuates

itself. Something's
in the branches that I can't
identify, half out of the water
— a longish bundle bound
with rawhide straps. I must
secure the tree, its wood
so rare and precious,

though instinct tells me
I should let it go,
that it brings death. All
migrations start with wood,
skop says, wood enough
to build a boat. Water's
deep; my only recourse

now's to swim. What closes
on my leg as I approach,
drags me under? I struggle
hard against the lack
of air. From underneath
the tree seems full of faces,
father's, Yold's, others.

My foot tangled in weed,
submerged branches. I know
this icy lover wants me
dead. I can't give up, my
face and mouth contorted
in a grimace. My hands
thrash out, something solid

to haul myself upwards.
Fingers clamp, at last,
on what they need, legs
kick free, my head bursts
gasping into air, blue with cold,
with birthing. Objects
I thought faces only shags

lifting off into the grey
sky. I'm being towed ashore
by Yold, his sister, my arms
in a death grip around
the infant cradled in its sack
of skin, skull the shape and
colour of a puffball.

How I Was Launched

Mother was a McGregor from Inverness,
a beanpole but ambitious. And tough as gorse.
She would not so much turn her head

as swivel her gaze so one eye peered at you
across the bridge of an aquiline nose.
My father was a short almost comic

figure from Exmoor whom she had met
while stationed in the Orkneys. She admired
the way he danced the foxtrot, swallowed

his vowels. His natural vulgarity
survived military service unscathed.
As a teenager I would nickname them

Jiggs and Maggie after the cartoon
characters, Maggie the great pretender
and social climber, Jiggs the constant

embarrassment with his top hat, cigar,
and bad manners, who was always ducking
out to eateries in Boston for a snack

of corned beef and cabbage. My father
finally persuaded her to sleep with him
in the summer of 1919 in a small cottage

overlooking Scapa Flow, where the German
fleet was anchored, awaiting the results
of the Versailles talks. She was sitting

upright in bed, the sheet to her shoulders
while he undressed, a cigarette in one hand.
As he stepped out of his bellbottoms

and dropped his underwear, not a bit shy
of his enthusiasm, she put her hand
over her mouth to suppress a scream.

Behind him fifty-four ships, scuttled by
defiant crews who jammed open seacocks
and took to the boats, were listing at odd

angles in the glittering waves. My parents
stood in the window naked, his arm
around her hips, hers slung across his shoulders,

and watched. He flicked a benediction
of fine ash on the windowsill, looked down
at his wilted submariner, and laughed.

Magnetic North

Midnight, my ghosts restless, wanting
answers. Scratches in the pantry. A deer
mouse gapes at me in the flickering

candlelight, dives for cover behind the oatmeal,
tail exposed. I press the tiny rope of flesh
between thumb and forefinger, deposit it

outside, threatening violence. No good reason
for parting. We always managed. First call
bagged two bachelors ambling awkward

up the gangway, oars extended
out behind their backs like wings.
At the foot of the garden, you paused

to wave, your body truncated by
runner beans. I leaned in the doorway,
throat dry, weak from anger, from fear,

stretched dome of my belly touching
the cold frame. Steam blanketed your face
in the frost, the half light. My saintly

gob. I wish I'd made peace. Lady Franklin
mounted a second expedition. By then,
I'd buried all hope. Journal pages, remains

of two men in a small dinghy. Sketches of a ship
encased in ice, hoarfrost diffusing a blue
light. Unmoved by history or the articulation

of private grief, the deer mouse makes a dash
for loose foundation stones. Back in the beloved's arms
before I draw the night bolt, snuff the candle.

Mon Petit Chou

I feel the sun's rays penetrate
the heavy canvas weave
of the tent, so air expands,
pushing out the sides like a loaf

of bread. Little good it does me,
feverish, swathed in wool
and cotton strips like a mummy.
How long has it been? Eons,

according to my clock. I'd drop
the *I*, but you expect subtler
expressions of arousal from scions
of nobility. Post-op infection

complicated by malaria. Wounded
pride is slow to heal. And you
must shoulder some of the blame
for being beautiful, knowing

how to move your body. That
night, flimsy garments, goosebumps
and all, you approximated divinity,
demonstrated the new physics:

such particles, such motion! Grace,
no trump. So besotted I packed
only umbrella and toothpaste.
I hope the neighbours enjoyed

the spectacle, though there were
no curtain calls. Or curtains.
Fallen angels recorded our follies
on film, 16mm, archival reruns

for lonely nights. We never climaxed,
our bladders too full. My fingers
recall your wind-sculpted dunes
beneath silk. Bless the arthritic

hands of weavers, clothing glory,
commend them to Christ and his
Celestial Management Corp, brokers
in desire, epistolary contraband.

Your previous letter, for which
my tortured soul journeyed
leagues, went astray in the Negev
under some putrid camel. Yes,

prostrate, like me, from love's
burden. *Assalām alaikum*,
whispers my Muslim brother,
while the embassy Chev waits,

scrofulous, in the brutal sun,
all but a few flakes of blue paint
gone, revving its sandblasted
cylinders. In Aden, mail delivery

contracts are auctioned twice
daily to the lowest bidder,
no clergy attending. You might
envisage cutthroats, a dozen

ignorant, unwashed chaps engaged
in a slap-and-grunt dramaturgy
as they desecrate your finest lapses
in discretion. Not so. The eyes

that scan your precious inklings
are darkly intelligent, perhaps
a little melancholy, pausing to wipe
a tear, or quote from some wistful epic

a line or two of verse. Efforts are made
to replace the seal, protect the script,
once it's obvious the orgasmic politics
are neutral. Stereotypes of Islam

bedevil our fragile diplomacy.
Even the Copts agree, we have
in English no vocabulary to describe
the Arab world, its codes, the value

placed on honour, on nobility
of sentiment. Faithful constabulary
are proof positive; so, too, my father's
driver, an old man who'd lost an eye

in Khartoum. He took his own life
for failing to deliver a dispatch
on time. It bothers me not a little
to think of the colonel's dull face

in Cairo. These people we betray
now the war's ended, they won't
forget. Yes, I know, it's reckless
to express in urinals of the all-

too-public post such thoughts.
My colleagues doubtless read them
first; then your husband, playing
Lord Fauntleroy in Jerusalem,

tying himself in knots while refugees
arrive by the boatload each night
under the Urgun's protection. How
did two Orkney lads wind up

marooned in the desert, dreaming
the same oasis? I resist my impulse
to expose his incompetence. The date
palm drops a taproot sixty feet

into the ground. For tuppence,
I'd sack the lot of them, these toadies
he dotes on. Relish your solitude,
private rhapsodies, as you take

the Daimler to the harbour, aware
of the slow leak in the right rear
tire. Since petrol is still rationed,
perhaps you'll go on foot, past

the Tea Shoppe, scones, butter,
assorted jams, pause at St. Magnus,
a faint flush as you recall my words
near the altar, how you stopped

and pressed my fingers to your breast.
Maybe you're in the back seat
with Thomas, his chauffeur's cap
wedged between the windshield

and dash, so the peak, at rest, dips
over the white dial of the odometer
that resembles my surprised, round
Orkney officer's face. Full stop.

They're securing all roads around
the perimeter of Jerusalem. I've
been told to turn the other way,
to keep quiet, but I know families

in Dair Yasein. T.E. Lawrence
was a fool, but he loved them
— the race, the language, the boys —
acknowledged the deception,

and mourned our breach of faith,
at least in private. While he wrestled
with his conscience, my father's
driver lay under sand, his life

in forfeit to a code. In ghostly
deference "Arabia" eased his throttle
in the English countryside. Your
epistle is frank, explicit. I thank you

for that. I never thought, as I explained
to Michael the day we enlisted,
that words alone could hold the stars
in check, but I loved the sultry

orbit of your hips. British arms, used
against our one-time allies. To hone
the craft was all, bring a little order.
Un viel histoire, n'est-ce pas?

What's to say? Bare feet addressing
four sides of the intricate Turkish weave
in my room in Kirkwall. How could
the soldiering heart not surrender?

The Calf of Eday

Carrick House, on which I'd set
my sights, dominates Isthmus Isle,
where the laird and his swaggers
all held court. My erstwhile

liege deserved no coin or quarter,
squeezing his crofters for rent,
living it up in the lap of Eday
smug as a sack of millet. Hell-bent

I turned into the wind my *Revenge*,
sails unfurled, prow beating
westward, the lads in fine form,
salt taste of success keeping

us focussed on the job. High
seas, low ceiling of cloud. We ran
in close to shore to avoid detection.
The seals had decamped, no fun

to be had on the grey rocks in such
weather. Whimbrel and storm petrel
snug in their shelves in the high
cliff, no retribution and vitriol

to be found in their so sweet
lingo. Lives lost trying to quarry
the same red sandstone they build
nests in. While shorebirds marry

and sing, human drones carve
yet another cathedral for the selfish
laird of the universe, who must
needs summer in Kirkwall. My elfish

lads and I, for such blasphemy,
would dangle in Wapping from strings
as the crowds jostle for a better
view. Collusion of God and Kings

explains John Gow running aground.
I made it to Carrick House, a guest
of the dungeon. A sleek rodent
crouches on a bottle of the best

Madeira, while fat cats patrol
the floor above. I've been irate
to no avail. Revenge is slow
work, except to hang a pirate.

Lovage

When she turns the car down the trail to Noup Head, sheep
flow towards her like spilled milk. At a nod from the farmer,
the border collie drives them back up into the shorn pastures
of North Hill, worries the heels of stragglers. Naught but rain
for eight months, the man says, his all-terrain vehicle idling
beside her rental car. Too wet for the grass. She inches uphill
in low gear until the flock disperses in twos and threes. Slim
pickings for all but the nesting seabirds. She can see in the
rear-view mirror farmer and son cross the yard, disappear
indoors, a gentle hand on the boy's shoulder. She thinks of
wee Archie Angel, clinging like a barnacle to his drowned
mother's breast, of others the sea holds hostage. Deep in
her chest, deeper than piercing cold, a love-ache. No relation
to *lovage,* or water parsley, an umbrella-shaped herb mixed
with pepper and coriander to form a healing paste, a physic.
Not so easily healed this one, like Balfour's besieged ego:
an unfinished castle, which she passed on the way from
Pierowall, equipped with myriad gun loops that neither
sheltered the Queen nor saved Balfour from the rope in
Sweden. A little violence, a little sex distract, for a time.
So, too, the pursuit of rare breeds. The puffin's antics,
shrill cries of razorbill and kittiwake. What does it mean,
this continual movement, binoculars blind on the seat beside
her? Vikings, surviving savagery and the sea, the whale-road
Crusade to Jerusalem, seeded desire in the barren Orkneys,
raised edifices, cozied up to God. Who could blame them
for turning from the sea's bitter harvest, seeking refuge in a
shepherd's hand? She parks alongside Noup Head Lighthouse,
steps out. Wind catches the open door like a sail.

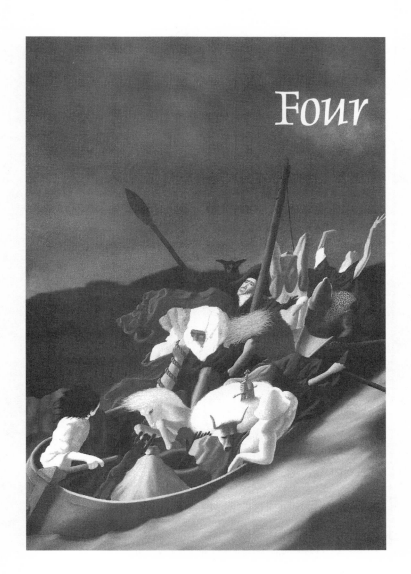

Four

The Zeno Transplant

First thing that hits my nose at dockside is raw sugar
unloaded from the *Chettinal Tradition*, huge jaws clamping
shut on the mound of crushed cane, drawing it up into a
hopper, to feed the clanking apparatus of the conveyor belt.
I leave my antiquated Sally Ann bike sprawled on diagonal
planks and settle down on a bollard to eat lunch. Lettuce
and peanut butter sandwiches. I'm not hungry, so it doesn't
matter. Inside the child's plastic lunchbox she gave me, as a
joke, is a Pooh Bear label on which she has written:

> For my darling, Nicholas Zend,
> on the occasion of his fiftieth birthday,
> Saturday, June 9, 1998.
> Abiding love, Dora.

Not Zeno, Zen. Antonio Zen. The final o came later, when my great-nephew published the letters that had fallen into his keeping, which seems to have entailed eating at least five and mangling the rest. I'd tired of domesticity and local politics and sailed north. Movement wedded to life. Wind drives you forward, passionate waters bear you up, wood alive and pulsing underfoot. Beached by storms, set upon by locals wanting booty, fearing invasion. Only the intervention of Henry St. Clair, Earl of Orkney, saved our necks. A hard man but not ungenerous, adapting himself to my whims. Birds, of course, were my first priority. Another, the presence of my brother Nico, who arrived belatedly with no loss of prestige. Nico shared my passion for birds and helped catalogue various species, skilled enough to sketch the red-throated diver's signature stripes, imitate the marauding merlin's strange capacity as mimic. You're a strange pair of birds, St. Clair announced; you scarcely eat and don't notice women. Not your typical Venetians. I assured him we were perfectly typical, that he'd tarred us with the Roman brush, an unwelcome stereotype. Venetians, I said, are like Norsemen, amphibious. Nico finished his flagon off in one gulp and offered to defend his honour in town, on the altar of St. Magnus if necessary. St. Clair loved Nico as a son and might have given preference among his daughter's suitors had illness not claimed my brother first. Nico took leave of the flesh in a strange mixture of pagan and Christian rituals. As fire consumed his body, Father Odred made the sign of the cross and read aloud profane runic verses that attributed divine powers to inanimate objects. This priest was a lover of anything that floats and considered ships the perfect afterlife for trees. He wept more for the soul departing those charred ribs of timber than for Nico's untimely demise. As my brother's keeper I had failed. Home was no longer an option. I set my sights and sails on the western horizon where others had ventured, where the evening sun distributes largesse, clothing the humblest creatures in glory. 1398, twelve good ships running before the wind, St. Clair never so happy. I'd placed Nico's finest drawing on the pyre, a kittiwake in full flight. The thin wafer of ash spiralled skyward on currents of inclement air.

United Grain Growers. Four lines run from the stern of
the *Handy Jade* to the pier beside the ATCO portable, where
the commissionaire lies, shirtless, on a deck chair. Suctioning
hoses dip into the single line of rail cars: prairie wheat,
Manila-bound. Folds of his belly radiate benevolence, like
the Buddha's. I have eyes, of course, only for Canada geese
congregating beneath the hoses, woolly goslings pecking
the loose grain under adult supervision. We met, Dora and
I, in unusual circumstances, covering the aftermath of the
so-called Peace Accord in 1993. I stayed at the Jerusalem
Hotel, a refuge near the gates of the Old City, its courtyard
covered in lattice and grapevines. Dora was there on her
own steam, six months of unpaid leave from teaching, and
needed to find cheap digs. I took her for a Palestinian. She
was interviewing peaceniks on both sides, including Yesh Gvul,
Israeli solders who refused to serve in the occupied territories
and spent time in jail for their principles. And Bedouin from
the Negev, protesting the expropriation of ancestral grazing
lands. Pieces that would appear in *The Straight* and *Vancouver
Review* and might have cost Dora her job at the college if she
hadn't been a Jew. Maybe it was the mottled sunlight on her
throat or the way she wielded her beer bottle to make a
point, but we moved in together a few weeks later, while
I edited my film on violence and creativity.

Father Odred, our priestly companion, often quoted scripture about the beauties of nature, making occasional reference to lilies, even birds. But he noticed nothing on the voyage and would quite happily consume these intermediate angels of the air. I described birds as closer to God because unburdened with human characteristics. Odred was scandalized, taking the view that all creatures are inferior and subservient to man. I knew his kind would rid the world of all variety, in God's name. The Greenland visit was right up Odred's alley — all monks and brothers, a blight of monasteries and stone chapels. Three weeks was my limit, thermal baths a consolation. St. Clair, as usual, busied himself with politics, trade, while I made notes on puffins, arctic terns, and a rare species of nesting hawk inhabiting glacial crags. I marvelled at the warmth of those woven, cross-hatched nests encased in ice. A man might do likewise, given strict control of circulating air, using body heat and a modest auxiliary source. The few notes I made on the subject were destroyed in a storm, sea chest inundated, my charts all but unreadable when we reached the eastern shore of what proved to be an island of inordinate size and abundance.

Other names tease my tongue as I cycle homeward. *Ocean Crown*, cargo indeterminate; *Sea Master*, a vast container ship registered in Rangoon but plying coastal waters between San Francisco and the port of Vancouver. Two rows of containers, fourteen across and five high on the afterdeck alone. That much freeboard an invitation to disaster, winds always seeking advantage: poorly stowed ballast, a too-high centre of gravity. Dora and I disagreed about Israeli settlements going up on Arab land. It's *all* Palestinian land, she corrected me. What difference do a few more illegal houses make? They can be part of the final package, make up for what was stolen in '49. My film remained in the can, not because of its poor sound quality, which could have been enhanced at minimal expenditure, but because we'd accepted tickets from an Arab airline listed in the credits. Too bad, as some of the imagery, the silhouettes of young Palestinian men dancing at a wedding, arms linked, was beautiful. And Loahez, interviewed about the time she spent in Israeli prisons. The exquisite torture. Dora even offered to mortgage her house to pay for editing the soundtrack.

St. Clair's vessel, scarcely three fathoms of beam, was low in the water, with an undeveloped fo'c'sle where trade items were stored and the Orkneyman and his modest retinue could take refuge. Odred, of course, made sure he was properly installed with his prayer books, out of harm's way. Work's, too. We'd come to depend on the rhythm of his raspy celestial interceding. I engaged him once on the subject of St. Francis the bird man, my solitary hero on God's team. He dismissed me with a wave of his ringed hand and pulled the rugs more tightly around his bulk: "Francis was a fool and an aberrant who mistook sign for substance. At seminary we considered his beatification a travesty, a joke. The only birds I give a damn for are those that guarantee proximity to home."

Six months before she died, Dora and I had just returned from shopping at the Santa Barbara market and were fussing over a small triangle of garden out front. Bent over picking strawberries, we heard the nasal tones before we saw the smiling face, dyed hair, and shiny blue pastel slacks: "You pick led ones, others lipen more fast." Mrs. Lu knelt beside me, laughing, and pulled several weeds. Then, in what I mistook as an act of magic, she took a black cloth from her pocket and unfolded it layer by layer to reveal a pale yellow love-bird of the most delicate hue, which hopped onto her wrist, cleverly defecating en route. Her old mother, all this time, chattered happily in Cantonese, as pleased with the weeding job as with the bird display. Wrapping the love-bird and tucking it away, Mrs. Lu patted her other pocket to indicate a second stowaway. "At home thlee babies almost old enough go for walk. Need lots pocket."

Pockets of fish, pockets of ice, as we set sail from Fortress Island. Dried
fish stowed in hammocks, salted and packed in canvas, or pickled in kegs
of wine that had gone sour. A few still flapping underfoot in bilge water.
Too much like work, Odred muttered, praising his harsh, ascetic northern
God for fair winds, but not for abundant sea life. St. Clair determined
to reach the coast of New Orkney in time to make preliminary charts and
construct his winter quarters. The runic markers we found confirmed we
weren't the first arrivals. One of the women invited on board was fair-
skinned and seemed less than surprised by our practice of using utensils
to eat or employing the mouth and fingers in copulation. I took pleasure
in showing her Nico's sketches. She reached out to touch one of them as
if it might fly off at any moment. I made my own rough approximations
of species of gull and waterhen, too crude, alas, to enlist her admiration,
but a record of sorts. I lacked skill to render birds in flight, though my
own life was one of constant movement.

Dora, a professor of Old Norse literature, used to leave the radio on to scare off potential thieves, a habit I scoffed at but have picked up nonetheless. She thought the sound of voices deterred criminals. I insisted it was not oral cacophony that drove them away, but bad taste, realizing the inhabitants listened to interviews and tasteless phone-in talk shows. Quality crooks are discriminating, I insisted. They deserve FM radio, something classical.

All we wanted was to satisfy our curiosity, not lay claim to lands inhabited already. St. Clair had no designs on history, no grandiose ambitions, only itchy feet. I kept my eye on the caged crows swinging from a hook in the foc'sle. They were green with mildew and looked so stiff from lack of exercise, I doubted they'd be fit to fly, never mind scout for land. The largest male flung himself against the wire mesh, cursing his captors. At night, I slipped them extra food and let them fly about on deck with a light twine about one ankle.

The afternoon-show host is interviewing an Israeli doctor, a transplant specialist. Animal organs, he insists, are too risky; they can't be disinfected against unknown viruses. A pig's valve is not a live organ and can be thoroughly cleansed. However, statistics on rejection indicate the procedure isn't working. The human body knows, by instinct, what we can't tolerate. I thought I heard a familiar name over the sound of my coffee grinder reducing frozen beans to a fine powder. I love that smell; better even than the taste of fresh coffee when it's brewed. In Dublin they crank the fumes of roasting coffee into Grafton Street once every hour, a fish hook in the tender flesh of the nose that hauls you in. An olfactory Pied Piper. That's when I heard the Israeli physician name the operation — xenotransplant.

I knew when the earl established winter camp in New Orkney, I'd
be the one to sail the remnants home, if I can use that word for my
adopted place. St. Clair read my thoughts. You owe me nothing,
Antonio. You're free to return home to Venice. Take Odred with you.
He ought to visit Rome before he dies. Besides, he'd be a nuisance
here, complaining about conditions and trying to convert the locals.
Venice seemed more remote than ever. I'd been away too long, my rough
hands viewed askance at table.

The plastic vial of medicine is where I left it on the counter by the radio: thrice a day at meals, plus an admonition prohibiting alcohol. Yes, vile in that sense too. You feel different about a place where you've buried a loved one. Chemotherapy has left me looking like a Buddhist monk. I find that part amusing, but not the nausea. I love to eat, keep nothing down except raw cabbage.

How Odred would have laughed. I teased him and the others about the quantities of kale they consumed, calling it domesticated seaweed. When we reached Orkney, he refused to make the trip to Rome, citing unfinished pastoral duties. I knew he feared the realization of his dream. And so I left him snug beside his hearth, threatening to copy St. Clair's charts and journals: a wise old owl, arthritic claws gripping the armrest of carved oak.

Since morning, nothing on my desk has changed. Not true: the light is different and minute particles of dust, mostly dead skin, have taken residence on my copy of Kay Jamison's treatise on art and madness, *Touched with Fire*. The paperback cover has started to curl from moisture and shoddy crafts-manship. A hard ship to navigate, that one. Jamison's crafty, though, arguing the case for poets as part of a manic-depressive elite, over-sensitive from being cut across the grain. Sexton's insistence: "Hurt must be examined like the plague"; Lowell's description of living with one layer of skin missing. He refused to think of depression as a gift of the Muse, but owned some good sour bitter work derived therefrom — acceptable, perhaps, "on sufferance."

I miscalculated, taking the fleet too close to land in order to elude the heavy seas off New Orkney. Cargo was clattering about, several barrels of fish broken loose, endangering lives. The crew bailing, frantic, unable to stay ahead of the water we shipped, thirty-foot troughs and, of course, following seas breaking over the stern. St. Clair's vessel, being two fathoms longer, had sufficient canvas to pull free. Mattis, father and son, knowing they could not clear the headland, foundered trying to change direction, all men lost. We found the boy washed ashore the next day, strapped to the mast as if crucified, his thin blue wrists bird-like, unbroken. I was incompetent, bodies mounting up to prove it. I forsook the helm and flung myself among smashed barrels and bales of skins. Nico's face and that of the younger Mattis stared up at me from among the pale heads of cabbage.

Next door, where the small stucco bungalow once stood,
are foundations laid for a new duplex. Cheaper to demolish
than renovate; and more revenue for the city. I lament such
ruptures, though I loathe the old crushed-glass surfaces, with
their deadly utilitarianism. Slick salesmen, taking advantage
of post-war fear and the low incomes of the poor. And now
wreckers, their crab's claw rampant, make room for what is
new. The aging owners planted, in good faith, a full garden,
beans and green onions trucked off along with cabbages and
quality topsoil. At least they're not around to witness the
travesty. My own strategies no less transparent. I exercise
daily, write myself lengthy notes to stimulate recall. Consume
what I can to delay the inevitable, spare my friends the true
picture of brain tissue wasting, organs closing down. CRAFT,
Peter said: it means, Can't Remember A Fucking Thing.

Orkney disappeared astern in a bank of usurping fog. It was as if my only remaining support had been withdrawn. That crazy, ragged patchwork quilt of islands on which I'd stumbled, run aground, had knitted itself into my thoughts. Knotted, rather. Now that the mooring lines are cut I carry it inside: Odred camped on an optic nerve, masking affection in a frown; St. Clair charting the thalamus, mocking my interest in birds, a true companion in adversity.

Last January in Ottawa, I photographed a dozen suburban shrubs wrapped in burlap against the winter. I called them "The Missionaries." A world encased in ice, wires and broken branches on top of parked cars. Ghostly, lunar, of no small consequence. Hit and run? It made no sense. She'd just presented a paper on gender stereotypes in Old Norse. I always loved the sandwiches she made, anything that touched her hands. Even peanut butter and lettuce. Hearing inconclusive, no charges laid. I paid respects, but couldn't leave without my two-litre skim milk container of ashes, bone fragments. Teeth removed and any parts that might be identified. All summer her tea roses smiled in gratitude. Soon they'll have one more reason to smile — the perfect transplants. We come bearing messages, authority; depart empty, scoured. Zero, not Zeno, not even the hairless Zen monk I catch grinning from the distorted foil mirror in the combination bathroom-pantry off the kitchen. He tried Buddhism, but preferred women and illegal substances. He should have spelled his name K-O-A-N. Ships, a baker's dozen at anchor in the outer reaches of Vancouver harbour, beyond Lion's Gate. One has just received a signal to replace the *Chettinal* or *Handy Jade* at dockside. Nearby, the grain-fed geese are bedding down.

Acknowledgements

I would like to thank the Canada Council, Concordia University, the Department of Foreign Affairs, and the University of Western Washington for moral and financial support during the writing of these poems. During the research and writing, I had the opportunity to attend a reunion in Kirkwall, Scotland, of Canadians of Orkney origin and to read my poems in the Stromness Art Gallery. To those who helped to make this possible, I extend my heartfelt thanks. "Skara Brae" was published in *The Bellingham Review*. Three prose poems appeared in poster form and in a publication of the National Library of Scotland, Edinburgh. Thanks to William Ford, who tripped the switch for these poems; to the teachers enrolled in the 1997 Education Faculty Summer School at the University of Victoria, who endured early drafts; and to Alexander Hutchison, Ron Smith, Robert Kroetsch, Henry Beissel, Tim Lilburn and Andrew Mitchell, for encouragement and advice.

To Laurel Boone, Susanne Alexander, Julie Scriver, Harry Chambers, and the staff at Goose Lane Editions and Peterloo Poets, I owe a very special debt of gratitude.

Gary Geddes is well known as Canada's best political poet. Among his Canadian distinctions are the E.J. Pratt Medal and Prize, the Archibald Lampman Prize, a National Magazine Gold Award, and the Canadian Authors' Association National Poetry Prize. International awards include the Americas Best Book Award in the Commonwealth Poetry Competition and the Gabriela Mistral Prize. His poems have been translated into Dutch, French, Spanish, and Chinese, and he has lectured and given poetry readings in a dozen countries.

A wide-ranging man of letters, Geddes has published many books of poetry, fiction, drama, creative non-fiction, criticism, and translation. His anthologies include *The Art of Short Fiction* and the popular *20th-Century Poetry and Poetics*.

In 1999, Geddes turned in a new direction. Formerly a professor at Concordia University in Montreal, he now lives at French Beach, near Victoria, where writing is his primary occupation. His account of this life change, *Sailing Home: A Journey Through Time, Place & Memory*, became a coast-to-coast bestseller. *Skaldance* is his sixteenth collection of poetry.